Springer Spaniel

Series "Fun Facts on Dogs for Kids"

Written by Michelle Hawkins

Springer Spaniel

Series "Fun Facts on Dogs for Kids"

By: Michelle Hawkins

Version 1.1 ~February 2021

Published by Michelle Hawkins at KDP

Springer Spaniels is the in the top three of the most registered dog in the United Kingdom.

Springer Spaniels are good watchdogs.

Springer Spaniels are a good choice as a family pet.

The fur on a Springer Spaniel is weatherproof.

Springer Spaniels needs lots of attention.

Springer Spaniels have a lot of playfulness.

Springer Spaniels enjoy retrieving birds in their mouth.

Springer Spaniels are known to be good around children as long as they were raised around them.

Springer Spaniels are known to be loyal to a family but extremely loyal to one person.

The bark of a Springer Spaniel is like an alarm.

If left alone, Springer Spaniels can have separation anxiety.

Springer Spaniels are known to enjoy giving and receiving affection.

Springer Spaniels are known as a very hardy breed.

The English Springer Spaniel color is either brown and white or black and white.

Springer Spaniels have a lot of stamina.

To feel needed, the Springer Spaniel always needs to be doing some type of work.

Springer Spaniel enjoys swimming and anything that involves water.

Springer Spaniel is excellent at retrieving items such as tennis balls.

Springer Spaniels are a breed not knowing for a lot of high energy.

The weight of a Springer Spaniel is between forty and fifty-five pounds.

The coat of a Springer Spaniel is waterproof.

In the Spaniel family, the Springer Spaniel is the fastest.

Springer Spaniel can be very stubborn.

The ear of a Springer Spaniel is known to be floppy.

Springer Spaniel enjoys playtime with their human.

A Springer Spaniel is excellent at hunting.

Springer Spaniels are known to have an excellent nose for smelling out items.

Springer Spaniels are very poised.

The eyes on a Springer Spaniel are very expressive.

Daily brushing is needed if you own a Springer Spaniel.

Springer Spaniel makes a great K-9 tracker.

Springer Spaniels are very energetic when they have something to do.

Springer Spaniel needs to be trained to socialize early on.

Springer Spaniel needs always to have something to stimulate them mentally.

In the spaniel breed, Springer Spaniel are the tallest.

Springer Spaniels have a lot of endurance.

Springer Spaniel enjoys being around people.

Springer Spaniel either has straight or wavy fur.

Springer Spaniel enjoys pouncing on toys when found.

Springer Spaniels are very friendly to everyone, even a burglar.

Springer Spaniel has been used with search and rescue because they find a scent and stay with it.

Springer Spaniel will deliver items with a soft mouth and no puncture marks.

Springer Spaniel are great at agility training.

Springer Spaniel needs to be brushed at least weekly, if not more.

Springer Spaniels are very protective of their family.

In hunting, Springer Spaniel are used for flushing out birds.

In the American Kennel Club, Springer Spaniel are in the Sporting Breed category.

Springer Spaniel are used in the Mountain Search and Rescue.

Springer Spaniels are very patient.

In the spring and summer is when Springer Spaniel will shed the most.

You will need to clean the Springer Spaniel ears weekly.

Springer Spaniels are very intelligent.

If you enjoy running, a Springer Spaniel is a great running companion.

The coat on a Springer Spaniel is thornproof.

Springer Spaniel enjoys being outdoors.

Springer Spaniel needs at least thirty minutes of exercise daily.

A Welsh Springer Spaniel cost is red and white.

Early training for a Springer Spaniel is the best training.

Springer Spaniel enjoys long walks with their human.

Springer Spaniels are known for their low hanging ears.

Springer Spaniel has an under and an outer coat.

Springer Spaniels are known for having large paws.

Springer Spaniel needs training early in obedience.

Springer Spaniels have a protective bark.

On average, Springer Spaniels live between twelve to fourteen years.

Springer Spaniels have an extraordinary sense of smell.

Springer Spaniels are very outgoing.

Springer Spaniels are known to be excellent in K9 work.

Springer Spaniels are known to learn quickly.

Springer Spaniels are known to be very easy to train in anything that you want them to do.

Springer Spaniel is eager to learn and please its owner.

Springer Spaniel needs to be socialized early.

Springer Spaniel needs to have their nails trimmed regularly.

Springer Spaniels are very easy going.

The best thing that Springer Spaniel likes to do is to retrieve items.

Springer Spaniel came to America in the 17th century.

Find me on Amazon at:

https://amzn.to/3oqoXoG

and on Facebook at:

https://bit.ly/3ovFJ5V

Other Books by Michelle Hawkins

Series

Fun Facts on Birds for Kids.

Fun Fact on Fruits and Vegetables

Fun Facts on Small Animals

Fun Facts on Dogs for Kids.

Made in the USA
Monee, IL
14 December 2023

49128425R00021